YOUR
HAMSTER

First Pets

Your Hamster

Your Kitten

Your Pup

Your Rabbit

First published in 1991 by
Firefly Books Limited
61, Western Road, Hove
East Sussex BN3 1JD, England

Editor: Francesca Motisi
Consultant: Nigel Taylor B.Vet.Med., Dip.Vet.Med.(Guelph) MRCVS

British Library Cataloguing in Publication Data
Motisi, Francesca
   Your hamster. – (First pets)
   I. Title   II. Series
   636.088

   HARDBACK ISBN 1–85485–082–2

   PAPERBACK ISBN 1–85485–173–X

Typeset by DP Press Limited, Sevenoaks, Kent
Printed in Turin, by G. Canale and C.S.p.A.
Bound in Belgium by Casterman, S.A.

YOUR HAMSTER

Written by Francesca Motisi
Illustrated by Peter Stevenson

firefly
Wayland

Hamsters come in many different colours! They are cheap to buy and they make good pets.

You can buy a cage from a pet shop.
A big, metal cage is best because
hamsters like to gnaw through wood!

You will also need to buy a food bowl, some special hamster food, a water bottle, a bag of sawdust and some hay.

Take a grown-up with you to help you choose a hamster from a pet shop. Ask to hold the hamster you like best. Hamsters like to live alone so you will only need to buy one hamster.

When you get home put sawdust in the bottom of the cage and some hay in the sleeping box. Fix a water bottle to the cage wall and fill a feeding bowl with hamster food.

Hamsters are shy animals and they can't see very well. Speak quietly to your hamster and let it sniff your hand. Then, use both hands to pick up your hamster and gently put it inside its new home!

Wild hamsters live in burrows in the desert. They sleep during the day when it's very hot.

At night, when it's cooler, they come out to look for food. This is why your pet hamster will be more awake in the evening.

Wild hamsters run a long way to look for food. This is why your hamster needs a plastic wheel, so that it gets enough exercise.

19

It's also important to give your
hamster things to play with, so it
doesn't get bored. Pieces of wood,
wooden cotton reels and old toilet roll
tubes all make good toys.

Feed your hamster once a day. You can buy hamster food from the pet shop. Hamsters also like lettuce, cabbage, carrots, tomatoes, apples and pears!

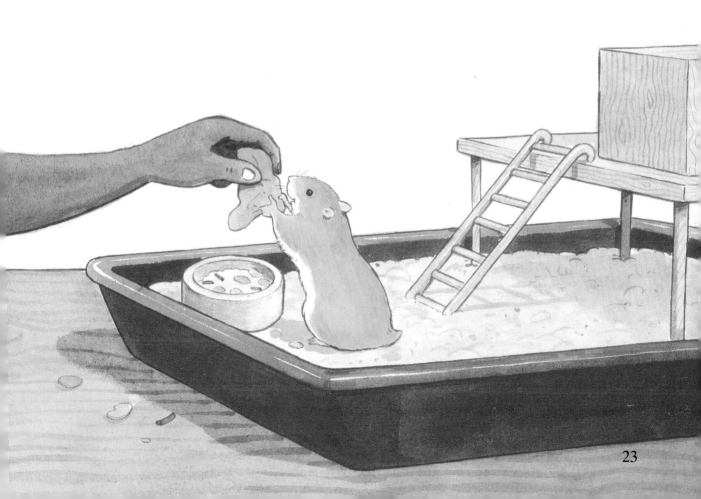

Hamsters don't eat all their food straight away. Instead they put it in special pouches in their cheeks.

Then they take it to their food store where they can eat it later. Hamsters also need fresh water every day.

Take out any old food and droppings every day. Once a week clean out the cage and put in some fresh hay and sawdust. Always wash your hands after touching your pet.

Taming your hamster takes time. Wait until your hamster wakes up before you touch it. When your hamster trusts you it will happily let you pick it up.

Healthy hamsters can live for up to two and a half years. If your hamster isn't very well take it to your vet for help.

It's very important to keep your hamster's cage clean and dry. A clean cage and a good diet will help keep your pet healthy.

The *Going Live!* vet gives some useful hints on owning a hamster

NIGEL R. TAYLOR B.Vet.Med., Dip.Vet.Med.(Guelph) MRCVS

Taylor's Tips

1 All pets need plenty of time and affection. Don't buy a hamster unless you are prepared to care for it properly.

2 Your vet will know where you can buy healthy, happy hamsters.

3 Clean your hamster's cage or rotastack out frequently. Damp, dirty cages lead to unhealthy hamsters.

4 Hamsters are prone to digestive upset if their diet is suddenly changed, or they are fed too many treats. Hamsters do like small amounts of fresh fruit, tomatoes and greens.

5 If your hamster isn't eating its food properly then ask your vet to check its teeth. Some hamsters' teeth grow too long and need clipping from time to time.

6 Always handle your hamster with care. They respond well to gentle, confident handling. Cup your hands around them to make them feel secure.

7 Golden hamsters can be aggressive to each other so they are best kept singly.

8 Russian hamsters can live together in pairs. Ask your pet shop when you buy your hamsters how they will get along.

Photograph of Nigel Taylor courtesy of Fast Forward Magazine. *BBC Enterprises Limited.*

9 Don't overfeed your hamster. Fat hamsters aren't healthy and often get stuck in their rotastack tunnels.

10 Sick hamsters respond very well to warmth.

11 Hamsters sometimes hibernate if their surroundings become too cold. Make sure the room you keep their cage in isn't too hot or too cold.

12 Always make sure your hamster is fed and watered daily.

13 Don't go away on holiday without making sure someone will care for it for you.